CHALLAH, CHALLAH,
for You and Me

By Barbara Bietz and June Sobel

Illustrated by Ruth Waters

APPLES & HONEY PRESS

For my sister, Elaine, and my brother, Richie.
Braided together, family forever. —BB

For Marcia, the best challah baker in my family. —JS

For the Tuesday crew: Wendy, Rachael, and Lucy. —RW

Apples & Honey Press
An Imprint of Behrman House Publishers
Millburn, New Jersey 07041
www.applesandhoneypress.com

ISBN 978-1-68115-666-8

Text copyright © 2024 by Barbara Bietz and June Sobel
Illustrations copyright © 2024 by Behrman House

Library of Congress Cataloging-in-Publication Data
Names: Bietz, Barbara, author. | Sobel, June, author. | Waters, Ruth
   (Illustrator), illustrator.
Title: Challah, challah, for you and me / Barbara Bietz and June Sobel ;
   illustrated by Ruth Waters.
Description: Millburn, New Jersey : Apples & Honey Press, an imprint of
   Behrman House Publishers, 2024. | Audience: Ages 2-3. | Audience: Grades
   K-1. | Summary: "The joys of challah, in all its forms over the course
   of a year"-- Provided by publisher.
Identifiers: LCCN 2023053097 | ISBN 9781681156668 (hardcover)
Subjects: LCSH: Challah (Bread)--Juvenile fiction. | Stories in rhyme. |
   CYAC: Challah (Bread)--Fiction. | Bread--Fiction. | Stories in rhyme. |
   LCGFT: Stories in rhyme. | Picture books.
Classification: LCC PZ8.3.B474 Ch 2024 | DDC 813.6 [E]--dc23/eng/20231116
LC record available at https://lccn.loc.gov/2023053097

Design by Alexandra N. Segal
Edited by Aviva Lucas Gutnick
Printed in United States

Apples & Honey Press books have accompanying activity and discussion guides. Download them at applesandhoneypress.com.

9 8 7 6 5 4 3

Challah! Challah!

Challah, challah,
yummy bread,
baked for you and me.

Challah, challah,
squish and stretch,
braided strands of three.

Challah, challah,
Shabbat blessings,
thankful for the week.

Challah, challah,
sliced French toast,
Sunday morning treat.

Challah, challah,
dipped in honey,
golden, warm, and round.

Challah, challah,
for my lunch,
picnic on the ground.

Challah, challah,
Noah's rainbow,
colors in each bite.

Challah, challah,
heart shaped dough,
chocolate chip delight.

Challah, challah,
tear and share,
with our family.

Challah, challah,
all year round,
baked for you and me.

From the Authors

Challah has been a special—and yummy—part of Jewish traditions for thousands of years. The blessing for challah reminds us to be grateful for the bread we eat. From classic braided challah on Shabbat and round challah on Rosh Hashanah to heart-shaped and rainbow challah, Jewish joy can be celebrated with friends and family on any occasion.

Wishing you a year full of delicious challah!

Barbara & June

Barbara Bietz is an educator and author of many titles, including *Apples, Apples, All Year Round,* co-written with June Sobel. She lives in California.

June Sobel is the author of the best-selling series *The Goodnight Train* and other books for young children. She lives in California.

Ruth Waters creates illustrations using collage, decorating the paper by hand using brushes, rollers — even old toothbrushes — to create unique textures. She lives in England.